PLAYGROUND PRAYERS

and Monkey Bar Meditations

by Rob Low

Published by:

FriesenPress
Suite 300 – 852 Fort Street
Victoria, BC, Canada V8W 1H8

www.friesenpress.com

Distributed to the trade by The Ingram Book Company

TABLE OF CONTENTS

This book is dedicated to my dad and mom,
Ron and Maureen Low,
who took my sister, Barb, and me to the park as kids;
my children, James and Brayden,
who keep me going back as an adult;
and my wife, Amber,
who holds my hand while I'm there.

"I tell you the truth,
unless you change and become like little children,
you will never enter the kingdom of heaven"
(Matthew 18:3, New International Version of the Bible).

PREFACE

In a world of adult problems, grown-up pressures and societal discord, there is something very powerful about having a simple, childlike faith. I think that's why Jesus said, "I tell you the truth, unless you change and become like little children, you will never enter the kingdom of heaven" (Matthew 18:3, NIV). In His wisdom, Jesus knew that the theological arguments and spiritual complexities adults often create for themselves don't do anything to strengthen individuals, communities or the kingdom of God. On the contrary, these seemingly important but divisive issues cause many people to lose hope and falter in their faith.

Perhaps it is time to set aside some of these conflicts for a while and take Jesus' advice to become like little children: to wonder, to trust, to hope, and to play. Children ask questions whereas adults would rather answer them. Children revel in mystery whereas adults feel more comfortable understanding, explaining and proving.

It's not that our beliefs are not important – they are. What we believe matters a great deal; it ultimately shapes our faith and our life. So it's not about forgetting these things altogether, but sometimes we need to shelve these things for a short period of time in order to marvel at the wonder of God and enjoy God's presence in a simpler, less cerebral way.

You can read this book while sitting at a park, spending time with a child, or relaxing in your easy chair, remembering back to your childhood days of playground play. Either way, allow your heart and mind to wander to that simpler place of joy and trust as you pray and explore the wonders of this great God who created us to play and worship in spirit and in truth.

COSY CORNERS

I discovered monkey bar meditations while staying at a retreat centre near Nashville, Tennessee. I love retreating and have stayed at dozens of centres across North America. Whenever I visit a retreat centre, one of the first things I look for is my "special place." Often it's the chapel; sometimes it's a bedroom; and quite frequently it's outside, perhaps on a prayer walk or a secluded spot by the water. My favourite spots tend to be what I call "cosy corners."

In fact, King's Fold Retreat Centre, where I lived and worked for eight years, was specially built with cosy corners in mind. Nestled in the foothills of the Canadian Rockies, King's Fold wanted every guest to be able to find a space for silence and solitude, no matter how many people were visiting. With this goal in mind, literally dozens of little cosy corners were created inside the lodge and outside on the pristine grounds.

During an afternoon of silent reflection at the retreat centre in Tennessee, I set out on my quest to find my special spot for the week, my cosy corner. As I walked along I noticed a children's playground in the distance. Magnetically it drew me, as if it were calling my name: "Rob, come play with me." The children had gone back to school after a wonderfully busy summer camping season; perhaps the playground was lonely.

As I approached the abandoned playground I looked around for the spot I would camp for the afternoon. My first attempt was the little landing area at the top of the slide. It was small and cosy: just what I like. But I sat there for a few minutes and it just didn't feel right; it wasn't comfortable or cosy enough. I then descended to the suspension bridge, thinking it had a nice angle to it that might mould to the arch of my back. So I lay down on the old wooden bridge and looked up at the falling autumn leaves... still not quite right.

Above me and to the left were some monkey bars. As I stared over at them I was attracted to their height and openness. This might make a good prayer spot, I thought. But how comfortable would those hard metal bars and the straight wooden beams be? There was only one way to find out.

I climbed up, wriggled around and hesitantly lay down, suspended in the middle of the monkey bars. "Bad idea!" was my first reaction, as pain shot up my spine from the bars digging into my back. I wriggled some more, adjusting where the bars were and finding the right spot to hold up my neck. "Wait a minute... this actually feels really good," I said to myself as the weight of my back sank deeper into the bars; it was almost like lying on a massage bed with all the right pressure points. After a few minutes of body-manoeuvring according to the messages my back and neck were giving me, I finally settled into an incredibly comfortable position.

I had found my special retreat spot for the week!

Each day I returned, and each time I got more comfortable as my body nestled itself into the monkey bars. I would lie for up to an hour with my back flat as a board, my feet dangling but supported and my head resting in just the right position.

With my body in perfect alignment to the bars, I felt I was getting a deep treatment massage. The weight of my body pushed the bars into my back, releasing all sorts of pressure. I felt my back and neck relax as the week went on.

The most enjoyable sensation for me was being suspended in midair. I was floating, a magician levitating several feet off the ground. With the sun above me, the leaves falling around me and the wind gently blowing underneath me I felt weightless, like floating on water or flying in outer space. It was truly a liberating feeling.

As I stared up at the big blue sky or rested with my eyes closed, all sorts of thoughts, prayers, and ideas began flowing through my head. With my body at rest my heart, mind and soul were released to imagine and explore freely. I began to realize this was what it was like thirty years ago when I played as a kid: free, fun, creative, restful and at peace. I had rekindled my relationship with the playground after decades of striving so hard at being a hardworking, mature adult. What a joy this was!

While my awakening occurred specifically on the monkey bars, I began to explore the rest of the playground, too, as a child would. I discovered other areas just as enlightening for my body, mind and spirit. Hanging from various parts of the playground stretched my back out in different ways. I felt an inch taller and ten pounds lighter. Swinging, climbing and sliding released positive energy that often gets squelched in our busy adult lives of all work and no play. The more I ran around, the more I discovered a world of playing and praying – and that's when I decided to write some of these prayers down for others to enjoy, too.

Ideally these prayers can be read at a playground, but these words can be equally engaging in your home, car or office. And, like most prayers, personalizing these words might make them more meaningful to you. Simply use these thoughts as guides and feel free to stray from the exact words, making them your own prayers for your personal situation.

NOTE TO THE READER

Like the Psalms in the Bible, these prayers are not meant to be raced through in one sitting; instead, they are designed to be savoured a few at a time. You may even choose to read one or two a day as an inspirational thought or daily devotional.

MONKEY BAR PRAYER

Lord of the Sky,
As I look up to the heavens I know You are there.
And I know You are here.
You are all around, living and breathing throughout Your creation.
As these monkey bars massage and stretch out my back,
You, too, s-t-r-e-t-c-h me in life,
Challenging me to grow into the person You created me to be.
As these monkey bars suspend me in midair,
You, too, sustain me, holding me up as wind beneath my wings.
As vast as the open sky is, so immense is Your love for Your children.
Thank You.

Help me to trust in You just as I trust these bars to hold me up.
Help me rest in You just as I relax into these bars.

Help me not to limit You to the vastness of the sky,
But to recognize You beneath me, before me, beside me and
  within me.

Help me to embrace the intimacy of Your ever-present Spirit,
And to follow Your sweet whisper throughout this day.

Amen.

BACK-ALLEY PRAYER

When I was a kid I could spend hours
Simply walking up and down our back alley.
There was so much to see and do,
Everything from picking up rocks to jumping in puddles
To checking out the neighbour's backyards.

There is something authentic about back alleys.
They're not as neatly groomed as front streets.
There are often leaning fences, older cars, weeds growing next to
    the garage
And unwanted trash items too big for the garbage collectors to
    haul away.

I try to make my life look like the front street:
Trimmed grass, flowers blooming and shovelled sidewalks,
Or like the front room of a show home,
Neat and tidy with matching decor fresh out of a magazine.

But the truth is my life is more like a back alley
Or a storage room in the basement
Or like that one drawer everyone has in their house
Full of odds and ends you're not really sure what to do with.

That's me, God.
I'm a little messy, a little quirky, and I don't always match.
My life isn't as clean as I'd like it to be
And I'm not as put together as I lead people to think.

And yet, like my back-alley adventures as a kid,
It's not all bad.
My unique personality is full of adventure.
My individuality is what makes me interesting and special.
I'm more like Grandma's cosy lived-in house
Than a showroom at IKEA …
And that's okay.
It's real.

Help me, Lord, not only to accept myself for who I truly am
But to go a step further and celebrate my life, my story.

And help me to go another step further and do the same for others,
To offer them the freedom to be real with me
And to affirm them and celebrate them for their unique reality.

Thank You for not making us all the same
And not expecting us all to be the same.
Thank You for Your beautiful creation,
Including the not-so-perfect person looking back at me in the mirror.
I will love others as I love myself,
And vice versa.

Amen.

BALL PRAYER

Kick, foot, hand, soft, base, dodge, basket, volley, racquet
Ball.
Soccer, rugby, tennis, ping pong
Ball.
Throwing, catching, kicking, bouncing, juggling, hitting
Ball.
So many ways to play with a ball.

Sometimes, God, I feel sidelined from the game of life,
Like I somehow ran out of bounds without realizing it.
But, like soccer, I can still participate from the outside,
Throwing the ball in to my teammates,
Then running back into the game.

I often give up too easily, lazily waiting for You to run to me or throw
    me the ball.
But sometimes I hear You whisper, "The ball's in your court"
As you wait for me to do my part.
Help me to recognize those moments when I have to step up,
Grab the ball (or maybe find it first)
And run back in bounds towards the goal.

Give me the strength to run, Lord,
With all my might,
Towards the prize.

Amen.

BALLOON PRAYER

Kids can be so easy to please.
I can give my son a simple little five-cent balloon
And it will keep him occupied half the day.
His eyes grow along with the balloon as he watches me blow it up.
It's as if every balloon he sees is his first,
Like he's never seen me blow one up before.
The look on his face is priceless,
And all over a silly little balloon.

He then throws it, squeezes it, pokes it, hits it
And chases it around the room as if it were a hundred-dollar toy.
The mind-wrenching squeaking noises from all the pinching
        and grabbing
Don't even bother his little ears.
He's got a big smile on his face while my eyes wince up
Like someone's scratching a chalkboard.

All is well until the balloon hits the stucco ceiling
And POPS!
Whether it's fear or disappointment
Or a little of both,
The wailing begins.
The same little five-cent balloon which brought so much happiness
        and glee
Has now been reduced to the biggest calamity
Since the morning's diaper change.

I can relate to my boy's crying, Lord,
Because so many of my life's hopes, dreams and plans have burst
Leading to hurt, disappointment and grief.
Throw in a bit of shame and a dash of embarrassment
And You've described me to a T.

Only my life's little bursts have cost a lot more than five cents:
They have cost me years of time, energy, money, hope
        and relationships,
Most of which I can never get back
And it hurts.
These are expenses I cannot bear.
I can barely admit them, let alone handle them.

And there is no one to come along and simply blow up another balloon
And wipe the tears away.

Oh, dear God, if it were only that simple.

I don't want another balloon, God,
Even if it's a new size, colour or shape.
Half the time I don't know what I want
But I know I need Your life-breath.
I need Your breath to breathe new life into me.
I need Your Spirit to blow life and energy within me.
I need Your life to flow through me.

Please God, fill me up
Because nothing else has,
At least not for long.
I'm tired of relying on things to make me smile
Only to end up with a big popping sound at the end.
I need something more than that
And I know it only comes from You.

Everlasting to everlasting,
Alpha and Omega,
I surrender.

Amen.

BATH TIME PRAYER

I loved bath times as a kid
And my children love them now.
They can literally spend hours in the bathtub
Playing with their tub toys
And just splashing around.

There's something about the feeling of water
Flowing around you.
Warm, cold:
They both feel refreshing
At different times,
In different ways.

I remember my mom washing my hair
When I was a young child.
So softly and gently,
Tenderly and lovingly.
No more tears, not just because of the baby shampoo
But because I trusted her careful touch.

The Bible describes Your voice as rushing water,
A flowing stream,
An overflowing fountain of living water.
I need that living water now, Lord.
I'm tired and thirsty,
Dusty and dirty in parts.
I need Your cleansing water to flow
Over me, through me, in me.

My well has run dry,
I've lost my way.
This dry and weary land has grown tiresome.

I long for a different home.

Lord, cleanse me, fill me,
Renew my heart
And refresh my spirit.
My soul pants for Your still waters
And I'm ready for the green pastures.

Splash me, God,
Soak me to the core,
Push me under the water
Like a Jordan River baptism.

I'm ready to be doused
By Your waves of mercy
Crashing over me.

I surrender.
I surrender.

Amen.

BIKE RIDING PRAYER

I wish I could say prayer was like riding a bike:
That I never forget to pray and just pick up where I left off
No matter how much time has passed.
But I'm afraid that's not true for me.
I forget to pray quite often.
Or I forget why I pray
Or the power in it.

It took me a while to learn how to ride a bike as a child.
First three wheels,
Then training wheels,
Then my dad running behind me,
Holding me steady.

Then my dad would let go
And I'd go a few feet
And fall on my asphalt
Over and over and over again
Until one day I could confidently ride my bike.

My prayer life is inconsistent
And my commitment to You ebbs and flows.
I confess I sometimes need training wheels
Or Your hand holding me and guiding me so I don't fall again.

I also need to learn to ride at Your speed
Rather than racing ahead with my own agenda
Or lagging behind out of fear and laziness.
To let You steer with me rather than me calling all the shots.

Help me, Lord, to remember You more readily and steadily
So I don't wander so far and wide.
I desire to bike in tandem with You
While enjoying the trail along the way.

Amen.

BUBBLE PRAYER

Kids are mesmerized by bubbles.
Start blowing bubbles on a warm summer's day
And you'll have your kids' attention for half an hour or more.
And they don't give up.

Even though the bubbles pop every time they get close to them
They continue to chase them, trying to catch them
Or at least touch them.

They demonstrate tremendous faith that one time, one day,
They'll be able to catch one…
… And they eventually do
With gentleness, perseverance
And, let's face it, a little bit of luck.

Blowing bubbles is an exercise of random spontaneity.
And trying to catch them even more so.
With the same motion you sometimes get eight bubbles
Or no bubbles at all,
Just a soapy mess dribbling down your chin.

And the bubbles sometimes float a hundred feet in the air
But other times pop before they even leave the wand.
They move like the wind
Or, more accurately, with the wind.

I have to admit sometimes my experience with You is like this.
I feel like I can't quite predict You
Or know what's coming next.
And I certainly can't catch You,
Goodness knows I've tried.

Your Spirit seemingly blows like the wind, too.
And yet, like the wind, You're always there,
But sometimes You're more obvious to me than other times.
Sometimes I can see You more, feel You more and touch You more
While other times it's a bit like chasing bubbles.

I'm not complaining, Lord,
Just sharing.
In fact, I probably wouldn't really want it any other way.
If You were too predictable and I could grab on to You
And even control You whenever I wanted
There would be no room for awe and wonder.
The fact that I don't fully grasp You
Is part of what makes me
Drop to my knees in worship.

I adore You, God.
I suppose that's more important than grasping You, "getting" You.
I honour You and Your greatness.

Thank You, Lord, for always being here,
Whether or not I see You, feel You or grasp You.
You may be somewhat unpredictable
But You're faithful and just.
I can't always catch You
But I can always count on You.
I praise You, Lord, today
And for the rest of my days.

Thank You, God,
For everything.

Amen.

BUBBLEGUM PRAYER

I'm embarrassed to admit
My two-year-old's first word of the day
For the last few weeks has been "gum".
It's funny how we get so fixated on things.
He can barely chew the gum, never mind blow bubbles with it.
But he watches his older brother and friends and insists on keeping up.
He can't stand hearing that he's too young or isn't allowed something.
It's like death to him – he hates it.
Throws himself down on the ground like the world has ended.

I lecture my kid for this childish behaviour
But then I turn around and do the exact same thing.
Oh sure, I'm better at holding my tantrums in than my two-year-old
But on the inside I can throw tantrums like the best of them.
When I don't get my way,
When I don't get respect,
When I don't feel like I'm heard or understood,
When I'm too young, too old, too tired, too...

My little boy struggles because he's *two*,
I struggle because I'm *too*...

Help me, Lord, to worry less about what I don't have
And to be more thankful for what I do.
To be less worried about what I can't do
And to be grateful for what I can.
It's not about "keeping up with the Joneses";
It's not about wishing I was younger or trying to be older.
It's not comparing anything with anyone.
It's about staying true to me, to my family and to You.
It matters what You want for my life
And what You expect from me and for me.

Help me to be less like a two-year-old,
Constantly measuring myself against the world around me,
And to turn my attention instead towards You and Your desires for me.
Help me not to throw tantrums every time things don't go my way
But instead to turn to You for the next step
And the healing necessary to get there.

I want to grow up, Lord, I really do,
But I get stuck sometimes in childish thoughts and behaviours.
I'm done with that, God.

Please lead me forward
To the good things You have for me.

Amen.

CLIMBING WALL PRAYER

Climbing walls are like my life:
Onwards and upwards with many obstacles in the way.
Sometimes I move too quickly
Without a solid place for my hands and feet.
I stumble and get knocked around a bit.
Help me to watch with open eyes, Lord,
To watch for the way You want me to go,
And to watch for the people and things You give me to hold onto
    for support.

Help me to keep my feet solidly grounded in You
So that I don't slip and fall when I reach out for the next s-t-r-e-t-c-h.
Guide my hands towards the good places,
The solid things that will hold me.

Amen.

DANCING PRAYER

I didn't learn how to dance as a kid, Lord,
I learned how *not* to dance.
Every kid dances; it's natural.
Children do not have to be taught to dance.
Kids jump and spin and bounce and twirl…
They dance.
But then the world interjects their judgements
And the dance changes.

I learned what kind of dancing was good and bad,
Acceptable and unacceptable.
I quickly learned what would get me invited onto the dance floor
And what would get me laughed off the dance floor.
I didn't want to be a wall flower,
Sitting on the sidelines, left out, all alone,
So I conformed.

The world hollered their dancing expectations at me
And the church echoed with its judgements
Of good dancing, bad dancing
And no dancing.
Dancing was suddenly no longer fun and free
But rather tedious and demanding…
Ouch.

It was so great dancing as a kid,
Not really caring what others around thought,
Though a part of me wanted them to notice,
To clap, to praise and maybe even to join in.

It was fun and free.

I didn't even care what kind of music was playing.
It could have been anything young or old, slow or fast.
It could be no music at all and I would just spin around anyway.
But I lost some of that as I got older,
As I began to care too much what others thought.
As I listened more to the outer voices rather than the inner Voice:
Your voice of love, truth and freedom.
I want it back.

I need it back.
You want it back.

Help me not only to sing Your praises but to dance them, too.
Inwardly and outwardly restore to me a stance of dance:
A way of living that is more real, more free and more creative.
Help me to roll more gracefully with the rhythms of life,
To sway more in tune with the song You are singing.

The Bible describes the sound of Your voice
As being like that of rushing water.
I think I can dance to that.
I know I want to.
But I need Your Spirit to set me free
And to dust off my dancing shoes
Which have been hidden away in fear and shame.

I have only one more question for You, Lord:
May I have this dance?

Amen.

FIREMAN'S POLE PRAYER

It's fun to climb up the fireman's pole;
Fun, but tiring.
It's tiring because it's meant to be slid down.
But the challenge is too tempting.
I want to show the world I can do it.
Just like the kids who like to walk *up* the slide
Rather than take the easy way up the ladder.

Sometimes I work against Your plans, Lord.
I purposely go the opposite way to try to prove myself,
To show the world what I'm made of
Rather than surrendering to Your will.
Help me not to see following You as the easy way out,
But as the natural and ordained way.
A way that works with the tide, not against it.

You created me a certain way for a certain purpose.
You fearfully and wonderfully made me.
You moulded me in Your hands and in Your image
And yet I fight against it, wanting to remould myself.

You are the potter, I am the clay.
I forget that too often and go my own way.
But I want You to shape me,
To form me into Your marvellous creation.
I want to flow with You, not against You.
To blow where Your wind blows.

Help me not to fight anymore.
I'm tired.
I'm done.
I'm Yours.

Amen.

FLYING PRAYER

Countless kids dream about flying.
The ability to jump off a roof
And soar mightily around the neighbourhood
Above all the rooftops and trees.

The dream of flying has been around
Since man saw the first bird.
Oh, to have that much freedom!
Nothing stopping you from getting from A to B.
No obstacle too big,
No valley too deep.
No wonder Superman is so popular:
Something in each of us yearns to have Clark Kent's ability
To leap tall buildings in a single bound.

Is it the freedom?
Is it the strength?
Is it the adventure?
Yes.

The Bible tells us we will rise up on wings as eagles!
Perhaps this is what it means:
Freedom, strength, adventure.
You desire these for us, God
And You equip us for them.

But so often the world has clipped my wings,
So I jump, run and hobble rather than soar with Your Spirit.
I know I miss out when I do that.

I often dream about flying,
And wake up just before I hit the earth.
It's such a natural thing to dream,
Such a natural thing to want.
It's my heart crying out for freedom,
My soul dying to rise above
The muck and mire of the daily grind.

Help me, Lord, to fly.
Help me to soar like an eagle,

To feel Your wind beneath my wings
And ride the strength of Your Spirit.
I long for this kind of existence, Lord,
And with You I know it's possible.

Amen.

HIDE-AND-SEEK PRAYER

Hide-and-seek was so much fun as a kid
Except when I couldn't find the person,
Or worse, when no one found me
And I was left huddling in the corner
Behind the couch under a box
For what seemed like an extraordinarily long time.

When too much time passed I began to worry.
"Are they still looking?"
"Are they still around?"
"Have they forgotten about me?"
I would begin to make small noises,
Giving hints as to my whereabouts
Without simply surrendering
Completely.

I know I do this with You sometimes, too, Lord.
I drop hints, sometimes even desperate ones,
Rather than just coming out of my little hiding place,
Showing You where I am and who I am.
I seek You in the dark, in the shadows, in the corners,
But I forget that You seek me, too.
I hide, seek and run all at the same time,
Sabotaging our mutual quest for each other.

"Here I am, Lord, take me, I am Yours."
That is the cry of my heart.

I do not want to be left in a dark corner any longer.
I'm tired of hiding, avoiding, justifying, waiting.
I just want to find You and be found by You.
Something tells me You're closer than I think,
Maybe just around the corner,
Maybe close enough to actually hear my breathing,
Like You've known where I've been this whole time.

If that is You whom I sense so close,
Then here I am,
Come and get me.
I'm ready to be found
And to show myself to You.

Amen.

HOPSCOTCH PRAYER

The hopscotch boundaries were fuzzy as a kid.
Drawn in coloured pastels with chalk.
They were wobbly, crooked and awkward looking.
Some of the numbers were drawn backwards or incorrectly
And the pavement was uneven with cracks in every square,
And yet I knew where to jump.
The parameters may have been drawn imperfectly
But it was clear where I was to go.
There was room for grace.

When my other foot touched the ground for a quick second
To stop me from tipping over
It was okay;
I just kept going.
When the rim of my shoe accidently touched the inside of a line
I quickly shuffled it over without batting an eye.
And my friends didn't care.

But now, oh Lord, my lines and boxes have become quite rigid.
The numbers are not only correctly drawn but all in the right order.
I get angry at others when they stray off the path, even for a second.
Mostly I get mad at myself.

Where is the grace?

What happened to the flexibility of a child learning to hop?
Oh Lord, I need a taste of that again.
Not so I can get away with things; I get away with enough.
But so I can be more loving and kind to others.
And to myself.

Teach me the way, Lord,
Show me Your path which is narrow, yet gracious,
Clear, yet flexible,
Set, yet forgiving.

I long for a heart like that, God.
Please massage my heart to be more like Yours.

Amen.

JUMPING ROPE PRAYER

When I was a kid I loved to jump rope
By myself and especially with others.
But as I got older I bought into the lie
That little boys don't skip rope;
They are supposed to do other things.

Oh Lord, how often I have listened to the world
Instead of to You.
How often I have listened to the outside voices
Rather than the Voice within:
The voice of love, joy, peace, truth and freedom.

Forgive me for not listening to my heart
And for not loving myself.
For not paying attention to who I am
And who You created me to be.

Heal me from those fears and insecurities
That cause me to incessantly seek the approval of others,
My need to fit in and be liked.
Deliver me from my weakness that does not stand up
For who I am and who You are.
Guide me towards a stronger, truer, freer way of living.
The way of living a young child knows so well:
In honesty and innocence.

Help me to jump towards You rather than away.
To jump with You rather than on my own.
To skip to Your rhythm rather than swinging back and forth between
Too fast one day and too slow the next.

Thank You for holding my rope and never letting go.
Help me to do the same.

Amen.

KITE-FLYING PRAYER

It's so hard to fly a kite
Without wind
And yet I tried as a kid,
Over and over again.
Running as fast as I can,
Throwing the kite up into the motionless air,
Only to have it plummet towards the ground
Like a crashing airplane.

And I admit, God, that I still try flying my kite
Without the wind of Your Spirit.
I pull and tug
And run as fast as I can.
I struggle,
Tossing my kite up into nothingness,
Hoping to make a go of it,
But it falls flat.
I fall flat.

Help me to stop fighting,
Stop running, stop pushing and pulling.
Help me to live my life
Empowered by Your wind
Rather than against it.
Or without it.
Help me to fly, to sail,
To soar like an eagle
As I ride the waves of Your breeze.

Blow, wind, blow;
I breathe in Your goodness
And rise to Your current.

Amen.

LAUGHING PRAYER

Studies have shown that all kids laugh.
Kids are not taught how to laugh; they just do.
Sadly, they are often taught how *not* to laugh,
Or how to calm down – or behave – or grow up – or act their age...
And the laughing stops.

Oh, to laugh like a child again,
Carefree, whether others are laughing or not.
Children laugh at the silliest things,
Often not even making any sense,
But the joy flows.

As children's songs suggest, we are to have
Joy like a fountain
Springing up from a well
And running over like a cup filled to the brim.
I want that joy, Lord.
I've had that joy, Lord.
I know that joy, Lord.

So why do I not always experience it?
Why do I suppress it
Or even kill it with all my analytical thinking?
Why can't I just laugh
Or at least smile more freely?

Help me, Lord, to laugh.
There is healing in laughter –
Science has proven it.
And not just emotional healing
But an actual bodily response.
Physical strength and healing comes with laughter.

Help me to embrace Your joy,
To celebrate You in the world around me
And to spread that joy to others
As I wear it on my face
And live it out in my spirit.

I want more joy, Lord,
And I know it's there for the taking.
I'm at the well;
Fill me up.

Amen.

LEGO PRAYER

Kids love Lego, God, because of three words:
Creativity
Variety
Freedom.
These words describe You, too, Lord.
At least that is what I see in the Bible
And in the world around me
And in the people around me.
It's also how I experience Your interaction with me.
My relationship with You is an invitation to freedom
And abundant, full life,
An invitation I too often fail to take full advantage of.
Your world is full of so much variety,
The diversity is outstanding!

I choose to be awed by it
Rather than fearful of it
Though I confess that fear creeps in
From time to time.

You call me to a life of freedom,
Freedom from the things of the world that weigh me down.
Why do I keep holding on to them?
Why do I allow them to hold me back from pure enjoyment?
I am both drawn to freedom
And scared of it at the same time.
Please teach me, God,
The difference between healthy fear that guides
Versus negative fear that inhibits.

I want to be free.
I want to be free to enjoy all You have to offer
And I want to be creative and joyful with my life
Like a child with a new bucket of Lego,
Exploring all the new shapes and sizes
And revelling in all the bright colours
As he digs around for the piece he's looking for.

Help me to be like that child, God,
Exploring life in a more adventurous and curious way
Seeking after all the goodness You have for me
And those around me.

Thanks for all the beauty You breathed into this world.
Help me to breathe it in more deeply today.

Amen.

MERRY-GO-ROUND PRAYER

"Round and round she goes.
Where she stops nobody knows."

My life feels like that some days, Lord.
Spinning around, not knowing when or where to get off.
Sometimes it's fun, like a child at play,
With lots of speed, excitement and variety.
Other times it's too much and I wish it would slow down or stop.

Help my head to stop spinning, Lord.
Give me focus and strength for the task at hand,
For Your assignment for today: no more and no less.
Help me not to spin around so much that I get dizzy and
Sick to my stomach.
But help me not to stop living altogether; I still want to play.
Help me to follow Your speed, Your rhythm, Your path.
When You are pushing the merry-go-round it will always be at the
    right speed.
But when I push with one foot on and one foot off,
Sometimes I stumble and fall.
Please keep me centred in You so that I move around evenly
And at Your speed.

Amen.

PAC-MAN PRAYER

Okay, Lord, I admit it, I'm 40!
I grew up in the days of Pac-Man,
A far cry from the modern Wii and PlayStation games and graphics,
Just a little yellow half circle awkwardly roaming around gobbling up
      white dots.
The graphics may have been plain and the sound effects primitive
But I liked the simplicity of it,
The mindlessness of a joystick that only moved in four directions
And a basic pattern I could mindlessly do in my sleep.

My life often feels like Pac-Man.
I'll be going along, eating my white dots, no obstacles in the way
When all of a sudden a ghost will appear out of nowhere!
I try to escape and flee to a safe corner.
Sometimes I make it
And You are there to repower me
But sometimes I get trapped between two or three other ghosts
And there is no escape.

I only have so many quarters, Lord.
I only have so much time and energy.
I know with You there is always another "second" chance
And I appreciate Your grace so much.

But sometimes I get tired of the chase and long for some peace.
3,000 years before Pac-Man, the psalmist understood being chased
      by ghosts.
There were no video games, but plenty of enemies, temptations
      and distractions.
Like the psalmist I cry out to You, Lord,
To save me, to heal me, to deliver me.

I'm tired of the chase.
I long for some down time
Some rest
Some time in the shadow of Your wings.

Take me there, Lord.
Take me to the place where there is rest for the weary
And hope for the broken-hearted.

Make me lie down in green pastures
And lead me beside the still waters.
Gently place Your yoke upon me;
I am tired of carrying around my own burdens.

I'm out of quarters, Lord.
The arcade is closing.
It's time to go home.

Amen.

PEOPLE PRAYER

Dear God,
When I was a child I liked everyone.
Boys and girls,
Black and white,
Young and old,
Short and tall,
Slim or large…
I liked them all.

But as I got older I was taught how to judge,
How to make assumptions and create distance
Based on appearance.

I barely noticed these distinctions as a child,
And when I did notice them I saw them as curious variances,
Not divisive, appalling things.
I wasn't aware of people's religious beliefs
(Or lack thereof)
Until I was an adolescent.
It just didn't come up in conversation very much
Even though I was a churchgoer myself.

It's not that faith isn't important;
It is.
People's personal faith convictions matter
And not all religions are the same.

But faith should bring people closer together, not tear them apart.
Faith should create more love, not more hate.
Faith should inspire hope, not fear.

Somewhere over the years I lost some of my acceptance,
Not plain old tolerance, but love and goodness towards others,
Especially for those different than me.
I became more judgemental of people rather than curious,
More sceptical of differences rather than intrigued.

Help me to be more like a child
Who smiles at people and talks to strangers
Before he is taught not to.

I cannot go back to the naivety of a child,
Nor do I want to,
But I can capture some of that lost innocence
That gives others the benefit of the doubt
Before placing my judgements upon them.

Lead me not towards wishy-washy tolerance
But to true love and acceptance.
You don't simply tolerate Your children;
You love them, serve them and provide for them.
May I do the same.

Amen.

PICNIC PRAYER

Children love picnics!
And why not?
The fresh outdoors,
The buffet of food choices,
The soft, warm blanket on the ground,
What's not to like?

I confess, Lord, I have become too complacent with fast food,
Quick meals inside, in front of the TV or in the car.
I get used to the same stale diet
Not just with food, but with life, work, relationships
And other things I just let float along.

Help me to enjoy life more,
To get out into the sun,
To enjoy more variety in my diet, my schedule, my routine.

I often hear the phrase, "Life's a beach"
But maybe life's more of a picnic,
If we choose to get out and enjoy it.

The Bible gives us an invitation to a banqueting table:
Your table
A table of abundance, freedom, joy
And so many other things I hunger for.
I'm hungry, Lord
And thirsty, too.

Please show me the way to the table,
The picnic of life.
Resend the invitation;
I am ready.

Amen

PLAYHOUSE PRAYER

"No girls allowed"
"No boys allowed"
"No _____ allowed"
Playhouses, clubhouses and tree houses can be fun places,
That is, if you're invited in.
There have been times in my life when I felt left out,
Excluded, inadequate and rejected.
Often the people didn't even mean it, but it hurt anyway.

My inner child still feels some of these wounds.
Wounds that go so deep I still feel insecure about myself sometimes.
The Bible tells us You are preparing a mansion so big
It has rooms for all of us,
Even me.
A mansion so big and so full of love there is no need for exclusion.
Not only that, but there is an enormous banqueting table
Full of my favourite foods.
Comfort foods.
Foods that feed both stomach and soul.

Help me not only to await Your future mansion
And eternal banqueting table
But to also live in that reality right now:
The reality that I am loved, accepted, forgiven and good.
Good because I am created in Your image, as Your child.

Help me also to share this reality with others.
To open up my playhouse to others who are feeling left out and cold.
To show others they are worthy of acceptance.
May my playhouse have an open-door policy,
Not a "no loitering" sign.

Grant me heavenly hospitality for myself and my neighbour.

Amen.

POTTY TRAINING PRAYER

My son is finally potty trained.
While it seemed like forever
It actually happened quite quickly.
He was able to train his body to control itself
In a relatively short period of time,
A few months.

It's remarkable what we're able to learn
And how we're able to discipline ourselves
As children.
As adults, however, it can be more difficult.
My son only had four years of behaviour to change;
I have over 40.

Whether it's potty training, smoking, gossiping,
Exercise, dieting, spending or whatever the behaviour is,
It's hard to change.

And yet
If a child can change where he goes to the bathroom,
Surely an adult can change behaviours too,
Even addictions and compulsions.

This is not easy, Lord.
I've tried and I've strived.
I've prayed and wept and begged for mercy
And yet some behaviours and thought patterns
Continue to haunt me and to persist.

Oh, to have the discipline and learning capacity
Of a child.

I am Your child, Lord.
Teach me,
Help me,
Lead me,
Guide me,
Discipline me,
Help me with my self-control.

I want my heart, soul, mind and body to be disciplined in Your direction,
Not out of control and limitless.

I desire to be selfless, yet self-controlled;
Free, yet disciplined;
Momentarily present, yet eternally grounded.

Only You, God, can bring these paradoxes together
To provide the wholeness I need to live for You.
Knead them together, Lord;
Meld me with Your healing hands.

Amen.

RED ROVER PRAYER

"Red Rover, Red Rover,
We call Robert over!"

Oh, how those words echo in my head
And heart.
The sense of anticipation of being called,
Being included,
Yet in the same breath
The fear of not being able to
Break through the human chain.

So much of life has consisted of those same feelings:
Desperately wanting to be called
But fearing I'm not up to the task;
Called by You, by others and even by myself.
I'm tired of waiting to hear my name
And fearing hearing my name at the same time.

I'm tired of waiting, period.

I want to run,
I want to run through the chains
To the other side
To the people and opportunities calling my name.

I want to live life to the fullest,
Not worrying about what may or may not have happened yesterday
Or what may or may not happen tomorrow,
But to wholly embrace today in all its fullness.

Help me, God, to listen and respond with boldness, trust and strength,
And to run to You like I've never run before.

Amen.

ROCK PRAYER

As a kid I collected rocks wherever I went.
Not even fancy rocks, just plain old rocks
From the back alley
Or the parking lot.
I didn't need them to be pretty,
I just liked rocks,
Lots and lots of rocks.
There were so many shapes, sizes and colours
In my run-of-the-mill back alley.
My pockets would get so full,
My pants would hang down to my knees.
My mom gave me a hard time for always coming home
With full pockets.
She'd have to empty them before washing my clothes
(She learned that the hard way).

Collecting rocks is fun
And playing with them is fun, too.
Collecting, sorting, displaying, polishing, painting…
So much to do with simple little rocks.

As a kid I never thought much about rocks,
Until the first time I found myself stuck
Between a rock and a hard place.
And now as an adult I find myself there regularly.
So many of life's choices seem to end up between
A rock and a hard place.
Many of my decisions seem to involve choosing
The lesser of two evils.

Life is full of dilemmas.

I often feel at a loss during these times,
Even when I turn to You, oh God.
And yet You have been described as
The Rock of Ages,
A Solid Rock,
The Rock of our salvation,
The Rock on which I stand...

All other ground is shifting sand.

I feel the shifting sand all the time, God.
It's all around me,
Even within me.
Not only does the sand shift around me
But I run around in it like a chicken with its head cut off,
Jumping left to right with fear the sand may sink or consume.
I wish I trusted more.

I know You are my solid ground,
The constant,
The source.

I don't turn to You enough
Or feel that solidity often enough
But I know it's there.
It's there in the deep places,
It's deep and solid,
Solid as a rock.

Please help me to trust You more
And to feel the grounded presence only You can bring.

Amen.

ROCKET SHIP PRAYER

Rocket-shaped monkey bars are hard to find
Because they don't make them anymore.
But when I was a kid many playgrounds had a rocket ship to
climb around.

Space is so vast and mysterious.
Even with all we know in the 21st century,
Most of the universe remains unexplored,
Unknown and mysterious.
So, too, is God,
The creator of the universe.

We have not found the end of the universe.
There is no end to God.
Where the universe ends God's hand is still moulding,
Moulding, holding, shaping, sustaining
Loving.
God is larger than the universe
Therefore God is full of awe and mystery, too.

But like the stars in the night sky
I can look around and see glimpses of God.
The universe is not just "out there";
It's here and now.
I do not have to travel out to the universe.
I am in the universe;
I am part of the universe.
So as vast and eternal as God is,
He is also here and now,
Close, personal and available.

The kingdom of heaven is at hand.

Amen.

RUBIK'S CUBE PRAYER

Some of my friends could do it, Lord,
But I couldn't.
Well, I probably could have if I put my mind to it.

I could have studied the books
Memorized the patterns
Practised day and night
And mastered it like some people did
But it just wasn't important enough to me.

I could easily get one side figured out,
Sometimes two or three,
But I could never get the whole thing together.
I admit I cheated a few times
Switching the stickers around
Or even taking the actual pieces apart
To impress my friends,
But I couldn't do it right.

Sometimes my life feels like this, God:
I can get one or two parts of my life figured out
And even make them look good.
But I can't get my whole life together.
And this time I know reading, studying
And memorizing patterns won't work.
This time I need more than that.
With my life I need true change
True hope
True surrender.

I need Your hands to move things around
So they fit.

I don't want to do it artificially anymore, Lord.
I'm tired of only having one side look good
Or switching the stickers around
Which are now losing their adhesive.
I want the change to be real this time
And only You can help me with that.

Thank You, God;
I believe You care enough to help.

Amen.

SLIDE PRAYER

As I sit at the top of this slide
I recall the many ups and downs in my life.
I've slid down and climbed up so many situations in life.
Sometimes I've slid down hard and fast with no one to catch me
Or break my fall at the bottom.
These times have hurt and I still have scars from these wounds.
Sometimes I've climbed back up too quickly,
Before the tears were even dry.
I was not ready to slide down again,
But the pressure of life pushed me on.

Help me to remember that whether I'm sliding down, climbing up
Or just sitting at the top watching and waiting,
You are there.
Help me to watch and wait a little more
Rather than feeling like I have to be on the move all the time.
Help me to remember You are always watching and waiting,
Watching out for Your children and waiting for us to look back.

Help me to journey through the ups and downs of life
With strength and trust.
And help me to offer that strength and trust to others,
Giving people a hand up the ladders and catching them
With open arms at the bottom.
Thank You for the ways You guide us as we rise and fall
Along life's hilly pathway.

Amen.

SLINKY PRAYER

Nothing's more flexible than a Slinky, Lord.
You can bend it, twist it, jiggle it
And it springs back to shape.
As a child I was more flexible
But as an adult I have become so set in my ways.
I am less open to ideas,
To adventure,
To people,
And even
To You.

I know what I know
And I like what I like.

I am comfortable with life,
Even with the things which aren't ideal.

I don't want to change.
I've changed enough over the years
With lots of hard work and sacrifice.
Can't I just rest a while?
I know You want to stretch and challenge me at times
But does this have to be one of those times?
I'm tired and I'm okay with the way things are.

I want to be more flexible, Lord,
But maybe I'm more like a Slinky still in its box.
A Slinky in its box hasn't sprung yet.
It's all bunched up and can't flex.
It hasn't even seen the light of day
Or the potential of being played with
And walking downstairs
To the amazement of a child.

Oh, to break out of these walls,
Out of this box,
Out of this hole.

Maybe I need more help than I thought
But I don't know if I'm ready,
At least not ready for much.
I don't feel ready for a steep staircase yet,
But maybe some gentle rocking and flexing.

I guess it would be nice to at least get out of the box
And spring a bit.
Hmmm...
Maybe.

I need to trust You with this one because I'm not sure.
But I guess even trust is a start.

I trust You
I think I trust You
I trust You.

Amen.

SWIMMING PRAYER

Oh, how I loved swimming as a kid!
The freedom, the warmth, the adventure.
Nothing bothered me back then.
I was just happy to be splashing around in the water;
It didn't matter what others were doing around me,
I was just content to be in the water.

Nowadays I can be so fussy, so picky, so edgy.
Someone splashes me in the pool and I feel agitated.
Someone even looks at me the wrong way and I can overreact.
If only I could enjoy myself more in the moment
And not get so uptight about who's splashing or jumping or diving
    around me.
Who cares if my hair gets wet or I get a little water in my eyes?

Who cares if I'm a little cold for a while?
I care, that's who.
But life's not only about me – and it's over so fast.
There is not a lot of time for swimming and splashing
In the pool of life,
I need to enjoy it while I can.

I have discovered I cannot walk on water.
It's not a matter of lack of faith, it's just that gravity grounds me.
But I can float, I can swim, I can dive and I can watch the fish.
I can even scuba dive and water ski when I get my courage up
And stop insecurely comparing myself to others around me who are
    better at it.

I'm learning more how to float, to rest, to relax;
To simply ride the waves rather than fighting them with all my might,
Trusting these waves are leading somewhere
And will dissipate as they head into safe harbours and calmer shores.
I still panic from time to time when I look straight down
Instead of towards the horizon
But I'm getting better at it.

Help me to trust Your waves, Your current, Your direction.
Help me not to fuss over the little splashes that get in my eyes and
    mess up my hair.
But when I find myself overwhelmed, drowning under life's pressures,
Help me to reach out for help.
There are people holding lifesaving devices all around me
But sometimes I'm too proud or stubborn to ask.

"In the beginning God's Spirit hovered over the waters…"
It still does.
You still do.
You created the waters, You separated the waters,
You created us out of water and dust,
Breathing Your breath of life in us.

My first nine months of life were in water
And most of my body is made up of water.
You offer us living water which I so desperately thirst for.
It's there; it's all around us.
It's there for the taking, for the drinking, for the swimming.

You not only walk on water but You walk towards me,
Calling me, inviting me, welcoming me.
My response is simply to jump, to dive, to float
Or even just to take a small step closer to dipping my toe in the water.
It's a start.

Quench my thirst, Lord.
Give me a taste of Your goodness.
Shower me with Your presence.
Cleanse me with Your waves of mercy and grace.
Lead me towards the fountain of life
And the river of gladness.
I long to bathe there
And fill up on Your goodness.

Here I go…
Splash!

Amen.

SWING PRAYER

As I sit on this swing I recall the folk hymn,
"Swing low, sweet chariot, coming for to carry me home."

Swing, swing low, swing high, and swing as a child … swing.

While I acknowledge there will come a day for You to carry me home,
I realize in a way I am already home.
For You are here, and wherever You are, I am at home.
Wherever You are, I am at peace.
Wherever You are, I am at rest.

You provide for me a home within Your warm embrace.
You provide for me a shelter within the shadow of Your wings.
Help me to be more at home with my own self, my own body, my
    own reality.
Help me to be more loving and accepting of the real me,
The real me created by You and loved by You.

Help me to extend this grace to others around me,
To be a safe and welcoming home to people looking for a place to rest,
To offer the type of rich hospitality Jesus modelled for us in life
    and death.

Thank You for the promise of an eternal home in the future,
And the hope of an earthly home with You today.

Amen.

SWINGING BRIDGE PRAYER

As I run across this swinging bridge it feels wobbly,
And yet I know it is secure.
It wiggles a lot, but it's got strong beams holding it together.
Sometimes in life I feel like I'm on shaky ground.
But I'm reminded that, even when things wobble a bit,
You are my solid foundation underneath the sway.
I can live in the sway as long as the beginning and the end of the bridge
Are anchored in solid places.
The bounces can toss me around a bit and I'll be okay.

Help me to run and jump and play freely in this game of life
Knowing that the One who sustains me is strong and mighty:
A sure foundation,
A solid rock.

Amen.

TAG PRAYER

Tag was fun as a kid.
It didn't matter whether I was chasing or being chased,
It was all good fun.
But as an adult it's not so much fun.
Often I feel like I'm being chased,
Not just by people
But also by pressures, deadlines, expectations
And other things that tend to track me down.

Meanwhile I, too, am chasing.
Chasing all kinds of people and things
I think will make my life happier.
Why can't I just be satisfied chasing after You?
Why can't I just stop, rest, listen?

Help me run *with* You, Lord, not *against* You.
Help me to run *towards* You, not *away* from You.
I want to run, I want to play, I want to live.
I want to do these things with You and with purpose.

Amen.

TEETER-TOTTER PRAYER

Dear God,
Sometimes it's so hard to be alone,
Or at least to feel that way.

I remember times as a kid at the playground, having no one to play with.
That was fine for most of the playground,
But not for the teeter-totter.
I needed someone to balance me off,
Someone to lift me up and gently let me down.
I still need that.

Thank You for always being here, always being near.
Thank You for balancing me out.
Your weight is far greater than mine,
Yet You allow me to bounce up and down with You.
Help me not to bounce through this life alone.
It gets lonely and boring bouncing on a seesaw by myself.

Thank You also for those You send my way,
The people You bring into my life to bounce with me,
To balance me off, whether for a short while or a long time.
Help me to look for people on the playground who are alone
And need a partner.
Help me to be more observant and obedient to those invitations today.

Amen.

TOBOGGANING PRAYER

I loved tobogganing when I was a kid,
Except for pulling the sled up the hill;
I always wanted my mom or dad to do that part.
I liked the easy part, the fun of going down,
Not the hard part, pulling it back up the steep hill.

I admit I'm still like that, Lord.
I enjoy it when things are going smoothly,
A nice easy ride where I don't have to push or pull, just coast.
But it doesn't always seem to work that way in my life.
I find myself being asked to drag toboggans up the hills,
And not just for my kids, but for others:
Adults, friends … myself.
And I'm tired.

Why do I have to carry toboggans up hills,
Especially for others?
Why can't I just have fun
And do what comes more naturally with less energy?

Why did Jesus have to carry His cross?
Why do I have to carry mine?

Yes, I know why; at least I know what I've been taught,
But sometimes I just have to ask.

Give me strength, Lord; show me how to walk Your path
Up hills, down hills, around corners,
Through valleys, through deserts, through meadows,
In green pastures, beside still waters …
I just want to follow You, even when I have to drag something with me.
Please hold the toboggan rope with me, God;
I know You can carry more of the weight than I,
But I also know You want us to hold on and walk together.
Okay, here I go …
Here we go …

Amen.

TREE PRAYER

As I sit beneath this tree I think of You, God,
With Your mighty stretched out arms offering shelter
And refuge to all who seek You.
You provide shade for those who need it
And a safe place to sit.

Like the fluttering leaves above me there is constant motion in
    Your kingdom.
There are so many signs of You rustling about.
The leaves crinkle together like a chorus
Just as Your creation sings to You in harmony.

I want to join that chorus, Lord, the chorus that sings to You
And moves to the rhythm of Your Spirit.

Amen.

TREE CLIMBING PRAYER

Climbing up this tree,
I'm struck by the strength of the branches to hold my weight.
Reaching so far and wide, yet firmly rooted into the strong trunk.
Each branch is different and each leaf unique;
No two are the same,
Just like Your children, oh God.

I am also reminded of how much of this tree is actually unseen,
Underground,
Providing a strong foundation
And soaking up the water and nutrients.
Help my faith to be well grounded too, oh God.
Help me to go deep like these roots so I can be strong in You.
And help me not to be afraid of climbing and exploring.

This tree looks different from up here than it did from down there.
Hugging the tree feels different than looking up at it.
Sitting on the branches is different than sitting under their shade.
Playing with the green leaves up here is different than
        waiting for them to fall.

Help me to climb up the tree of life
So I can gain different experiences,
Different perspectives.

Help me to explore my faith just like I climb a tree:
Inch by inch, branch by branch, one step at a time,
Until I see the tree more fully.

Thank You for trees.

Amen.

YO-YO PRAYER

Up and down
Around and around
Spinning and bouncing
All over the town.
When did my life become like this, Lord?
And, more importantly, who can I blame?
I want to blame someone:
You or my kids or my work
Or the world in general.
There must be someone to blame for this way I'm feeling.

"Walk the Dog"
"Around the Moon"
"Rock the Cradle"

There are ways of controlling a yo-yo
Ways of turning the spinning energy
Into a pattern that serves a purpose.
It takes control, stillness.
These moves done too quickly
Or with jutting motions
Result in a quick demise
And having to start over.

But a controlled, concise switch
In the yo-yo's movement
Shapes it into what we want.
We suddenly control the yo-yo
Rather than the yo-yo controlling us.
It's a subtle yet crucial distinction.

My head is spinning, Lord,
My life is spinning.
It may not be out of control but it's not ideal either.
I settle for "not out of control"
Rather than living out of
Peace, joy, balance and abundance.

I invite You to control my spinning centre,
Direct the energy into a pleasing pattern.
Pull the string gently enough not to jar
But firmly enough to instigate change.

I am Yours.
Use me.

Amen.

ZIP LINE PRAYER

Lord, sometimes it's hard to take the leap.
Even with someone there holding on to me
Jumping off just seems too hard.
Will I make it all the way across?
Will I fall off halfway?
Will I look weak and foolish to onlookers?

Help me to risk, Lord.
Help me to remember You are the one holding on to me.
Help me to remember not only are You holding on to me,
But You *are* the zip line, the handles and the final resting place
All in one.

You are the Great I Am!

But I confess sometimes I need a little push.
Push me, Lord, gently, but push me.

Amen.

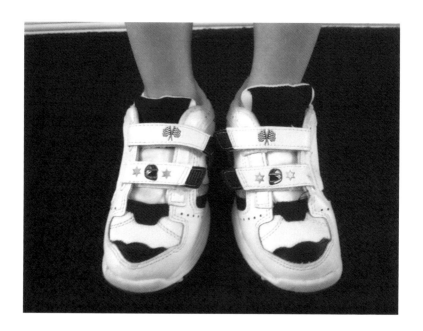

THE WRONG FOOT

On the way to the playground one day,
My son put his shoes on the wrong feet (as usual).
The first words through my head were,
"Son, you've got your shoes on the wrong feet."
But the words did not leave my mouth as my second thought was,
"Does it really matter?
He doesn't seem to mind and doesn't even notice,
So who cares; why bother him with it?"

But then my third thought kicked in:
He may not notice for the first several minutes,
But after running and jumping for an hour, his feet may start to hurt.
As his feet grow bigger and the shoes fit more snugly,
They may even damage his feet.
As his parent, I should continue to teach him
The proper way to put on shoes.

I proceeded to correct him delicately
And helped him switch his shoes.

This somewhat trivial moment made me think
How many people live their whole life with the wrong shoes on.
Many people go through life
In an unfulfilling relationship,
A job that's not quite the right fit,
An attitude that could use correcting
And other life factors which just don't line up.

Like my four-year-old with his shoes on backwards,
They don't really notice
And they seem to make it work,
At least for a while.
But in the long run
They would have been better off
Switching shoes
And making things right.

Who wants to merely *survive* with shoes (or lives)
That work and don't pinch *too* much
When they could be dancing
In comfortable shoes
On the proper feet
And enjoying a life that reflects
Their passions and priorities?

Oh, Lord, place my feet in the right shoes.

Amen.

REMINDERS TO PRAY

Many people struggle with prayer. Our memories are short and our minds wander. As a visual person I find it helpful to use images to help remind me to pray and focus my prayers. Next time you drive by a playground, consider praying for the children in your life. When you see a school zone sign, don't just slow down: slow down and pray for the students, teachers and administrators in that school.

Our children need our prayers, regardless of their age. Our neighbours' children need our prayers, and children we don't even know at the school down the street need our prayers.

Use these signs as reminders to call out to God and reach out to others.

LOOK LEFT, LOOK RIGHT

The other day I was taking my boys for a walk and it's always a challenge when it's time to cross the street. James is old enough that he's now pretty careful and safe crossing the street, but Brayden still does what James did when he was three. He shakes his head vigorously back and forth because I always harp on him to look both ways for cars. He's going through the motions but not actually looking. So I said to him, "Brayden, it's not good enough just to shake your head back and forth, you need to actually look."

As the words came out of my mouth, I realized how much I do this with God. I look around frantically for Him, moving my head, asking questions, talking to others and desperately seeking – but am I really looking? Am I really listening? Am I in tune at all?

Seeking God isn't about going through the motions, like my little boy crossing the street. It's not about frantically grasping at straws hoping to spot Him as He races by. No; seeking God is about watching, waiting, listening and hearing. It's about stilling yourself so you can actually see what's around you, like we adults do before crossing a street.

Many verses in the Bible encourage us to open our eyes and ears, implying God may already be in our midst but we're just not getting it. I would say this is often the case with me and perhaps with you, too.

> "Keep on asking, and you will be given what you ask for. Keep on looking, and you will find. Keep on knocking, and the door will be opened. For everyone who asks, receives. Everyone who seeks, finds. And the door is opened to everyone who knocks" (Matthew 7:7–8, New Living Translation).

WHERE DID YOU GO?

My son and I were playing at the playground on a warm summer's day when it was time to go home for supper. I asked him several times to stop what he was doing, get off the playground and follow me home. Like a typical three-year-old he kept playing, not wishing to leave at this time. I had never tried this before but had seen other parents do it so I decided to experiment by walking away to see if he would eventually follow me. I gave him the warning, "Okay, James, I'm leaving right now..." and I walked away.

I did not get more than ten yards down the block when I heard him running towards me, wailing his little heart out. I turned around and welcomed him into my open arms to quench his tears.

"You left me, Daddy!" he cried.

"I did not leave you," I replied. "I told you I was walking this way but you didn't follow."

As I heard the words coming out of my mouth, I was struck by this profound but simple playground moment. Many people lament a God who supposedly leaves, or was maybe never there in the first place. They do not sense God's presence and have not for a long time, or maybe never have. Or they do not sense God has played any role in their life – certainly not a positive role if they've lived a very difficult life full of disappointment and hurt.

While it is understandable that people would feel like God has abandoned them for whatever reason, I have come to believe it is we who choose not to follow God in the direction He is leading. God gives us promptings, feelings, convictions, warnings, instincts and intuitions which many of us have become skilled at ignoring. God also speaks to us in countless other ways such as through people, music, art, dreams, and books but, like my three-year-old, we get caught up in what we're doing and ignore God's invitation to move forward and walk in His direction. God does not just randomly walk away from us; God invites us and continues to wave us forward with open arms, no matter how far down the block we get (we're never out of His sight). We are God's precious children; we are always invited to experience His warm, parental embrace.

Where is God leading you now?
And where are you going?

"He returned home to his father. And while he was still a long distance away, his father saw him coming. Filled with love and compassion, he ran to his son, embraced him, and kissed him" (Luke 15:20, NLT).

CPSIA information can be obtained
at www.ICGtesting.com
Printed in the USA
LVIW011820031112

305728LV00001B

* 9 7 8 1 7 7 0 9 7 8 8 8 1 *